Original title:
When I Look Back

Copyright © 2024 Swan Charm
All rights reserved.

Author: Lan Donne
ISBN HARDBACK: 978-9916-79-126-4
ISBN PAPERBACK: 978-9916-79-127-1
ISBN EBOOK: 978-9916-79-140-0

A Testament to the Roads Travelled

In the quiet dawn, I lift my gaze,
To the paths before, in the morning haze.
With faithful steps, I tread the ground,
In every heartbeat, Thy love is found.

Oh, the hills I've climbed, and the valleys low,
Each winding road, where Thy spirit flows.
Through trials faced, and storms that roar,
Thy grace, my guide, forevermore.

In the light of dusk, I seek my rest,
To reflect on journeys, in my quest.
Every shadow cast, now a tale to tell,
Of the strength bestowed, where I fell.

With footsteps wise, and a soul so frail,
I journey forth, through every gale.
For in the struggle, I find my song,
In faith, I stand, where I belong.

So here I stand, with arms held wide,
In reverence to the paths I stride.
Forever grateful for the way I'm led,
In each road travelled, Thy love is spread.

The Tapestry of Trials and Triumphs

In shadows deep, we wander wide,
With faith as our unwavering guide.
The threads of hardship intertwine,
We rise from ashes, hearts divine.

Each challenge faced, a lesson learned,
Through storms of life, our spirits yearned.
From tears shed forth, the strength we gain,
In every loss, there's beauty's reign.

So hold your head and raise your hand,
In unity, together we stand.
For every trial, a triumph's song,
In struggle's embrace, we all belong.

Pilgrimage Through Time's Hallowed Hall

We journey forth on sacred ground,
Where echoes of the past abound.
Each step we take, a prayer unfolds,
In hallowed halls, the truth it molds.

From ancient texts to whispers light,
Our hearts ignite with love's pure sight.
In pilgrim's garb, we seek the flame,
A soul's ascent, forever claim.

With every footfall, wisdom grows,
In shadows cast, divinity shows.
The path may bend, yet faith remains,
In time's embrace, our hope sustains.

Moments Adorned with Celestial Hands

In quiet moments, grace descends,
Celestial hands, our hearts it mends.
In whispered prayers and silent awe,
We find the peace in love's sweet law.

With each dawn's light, a gift bestowed,
In nature's splendor, joy's abode.
A fleeting glance, a gentle sigh,
In every breath, the spirit's high.

Embrace the now, let worries cease,
For in these moments, find your peace.
In love's embrace, we find our way,
With every heartbeat, grace will stay.

Illuminated by Reverence's Glow

In sacred light, our spirits soar,
Illuminated by love's encore.
With every dawn, a promise made,
In reverence, foundations laid.

We gather close, in humble prayer,
To seek the truth with hearts laid bare.
As stars above reflect our plight,
In unity, we chase the light.

Through trials faced, our courage shines,
In shadows cast, the light aligns.
With hearts ablaze, we walk the road,
Illuminated by faith's abode.

Beneath the Watchful Eyes of Saints

Beneath the watchful eyes of saints,
Guiding us through trials and pains.
In every whisper, truth remains,
Their gentle grace, our hearts regain.

With fervent prayers, our souls unite,
In shadows deep, they bring us light.
A sacred bond, pure and bright,
In faith we walk, our path ignites.

The statues stand, with arms extended,
Offering peace, us they've befriended.
Their silent words, love's tale intended,
In every heart, their warmth suspended.

With every step, their presence near,
A steady hand when faced with fear.
In holy love, we persevere,
In faith's embrace, we hold them dear.

The journey long, yet never lone,
In every prayer, their love is shown.
Beneath the watchful eyes, we've grown,
To heaven's grace, our hearts are sewn.

The Prism of Past Lessons

Through trials faced, we seek to learn,
A prism bright where wisdom burns.
In every heartache, faith returns,
Reflecting light in sacred turns.

The lessons carved in time's deep trace,
Guide weary souls to find their place.
In different hues, we see His grace,
Embracing love in warm embrace.

Each stumble turns to light's design,
In shadows cast, His love aligns.
Through every tear, His joy defines,
A path created, pure and fine.

With every step, we grow more wise,
In quiet moments, truth belies.
The past may fade, but faith still ties,
Our spirits soar, like holy skies.

The prism glows, a guiding flame,
In life's vast tapestry, we claim.
For every lesson shapes our name,
In gratitude, we sing His fame.

A Pilgrim's Reverie in the Light of Faith

A pilgrim's heart beats bold and free,
In lands unknown, he seeks to see.
With each sunrise, his spirit's plea,
In light of faith, he yearns to be.

The road behind, a tale unfurled,
With every step, his dreams are twirled.
In silent woods, God's love is hurled,
A compass set in a waiting world.

Through valleys low and mountains high,
He finds his strength in each new sigh.
In sacred whispers, never shy,
He lifts his gaze towards the sky.

Each footprint left, a sacred trace,
In heart of hearts, he finds his place.
The journey shared, a holy grace,
A pilgrimage to love's embrace.

In every moment, faith ignites,
With every star that fills the nights.
A pilgrim's dream, through love's delights,
In endless joy, his spirit flights.

Reflections in the Mirror of Eternity

In silence deep, we find our truth,
Reflections dance in depths of youth.
In every heart, the spirit's proof,
Eternity calls, a sacred sleuth.

The mirror shows our fleeting days,
In every shadow, light decays.
Yet through it all, His love displays,
A path of grace in countless ways.

Our choices weave a tapestry,
In threads of fate, divinity.
In moments lost, we seek to be,
Eternal souls, forever free.

With every gaze, we glimpse the past,
In echoes soft, the die is cast.
Yet in this now, forever vast,
We feel His love, a bond to last.

Reflections sound, a holy chime,
In every heart, we rise through time.
Eternity's song, a love sublime,
In sacred truth, in Him we climb.

Sacred Reflections at Heaven's Gate

Beneath the arch of sky so wide,
We gather dreams the Angels guide.
In whispers soft, the heart takes flight,
At Heaven's gate, we seek the light.

With faith as gold, our souls unite,
In prayerful pause, we face the night.
Each tear a pearl, each joy a song,
In sacred space, where we belong.

The breath of hope, a gentle hue,
In every heart, His love shines through.
As clouds depart and stars align,
We praise the path, divinely fine.

In quietude, His voice we hear,
A melody that draws us near.
As shadows fade, and dawn appears,
We walk in grace, releasing fears.

The Pilgrim's Gratitude for Trials Faced

Upon this road, my burdens weigh,
Each stumble guides my steps to pray.
In trials fierce, strength is revealed,
A heart of gratitude concealed.

Through storms and flames, I find my way,
A softened spirit learns to stay.
The path of thorns, a sacred ground,
In every wound, His love is found.

Oh, Pilgrim's heart, embrace the strife,
For in each trial, blooms deep life.
With every tear, a lesson learned,
In gratitude, my spirit turned.

With open hands, I lift my praise,
For all the nights and weary days.
The journey long, yet sweet the grace,
In faith's embrace, I find my place.

Traces of the Divine in Our History

In ancient scrolls, the stories weave,
Of sacred hearts who chose to believe.
From prophets bold to kings of old,
Their whispered truths, as ages told.

Through trials passed, they paved the way,
In shadows deep, they chose to stay.
The echoes of their faith resound,
In every heartbeat, love is found.

The sands of time, where footprints lie,
Mark journeys led by the Most High.
Each moment held, a chance to see,
The threads of grace in history.

As dawns arise and dusk descends,
We trace the love that never ends.
From age to age, His hand will guide,
In every heart, He'll abide.

Litanies of Reflection Beneath the Canopy of Stars

Beneath this sky, a vast expanse,
We lift our hearts and join the dance.
In litanies of joy and strife,
We find the rhythm of our life.

The stars, like candles, softly glow,
A testament of love bestow.
In silent night, our prayers ascend,
With every moment, we transcend.

The universe, a sacred hymn,
In whispered winds, we learn to swim.
Each twinkling light a memory,
Of love divine, eternally.

As constellations guide our dream,
We journey forth, His grace a theme.
In every heart, a spark ignites,
Beneath the stars, our hope ignites.

The Path of Providence Laid Bare

In shadows deep, where whispers dwell,
The path of grace, we tread so well.
Each step adorned by fate's kind hand,
A tapestry of love, so grand.

With every trial, a lesson learned,
In darkest nights, a spark we've earned.
The purpose clear, though veiled in grace,
We find our strength in each embrace.

Through winding roads, the heart must roam,
In every storm, a guide leads home.
Together bound by faith's strong tether,
We journey forth, through every weather.

Divine the moments, intricately spun,
In silent prayers, the battles won.
With hope our shield, we face the day,
In love's warm light, we find our way.

Illuminated Moments of Collective Grace

In gathering light, our spirits rise,
In harmony, we touch the skies.
A chorus sweet, our voices blend,
In unity, our hearts shall mend.

The sacred bond, a gift we share,
In every smile, love's gentle flare.
Together strong, we lift each heart,
In moments bright, we play our part.

As whispered prayers take flight transcendent,
In every heart, a love resplendent.
With open arms, we welcome grace,
In the embrace of this holy space.

Reflecting light in darkest plight,
With every step, we seek the right.
Through trials faced, our faith ignites,
In love's embrace, our hope unites.

Guardian Angels in Memory's Embrace

In shadows cast by days long past,
Guardian angels, their presence lasts.
Through whispered thoughts and gentle sighs,
In memory's warmth, their spirit flies.

They guide our hearts with tender care,
In every challenge, they're always there.
Their wings surround in silent prayer,
A beacon bright, in love affair.

As dawns emerge, their light does shine,
In each lost moment, a spark divine.
Through endless time, their voices call,
In memories cherished, we rise, we fall.

With every tear, their love persists,
In every joy, their light exists.
They walk beside, in stillness stand,
Guardian angels, forever hand in hand.

Hallowed Moments Stitched in Time

In sacred hours when silence dwells,
Time pauses soft, a wish compels.
Each fleeting glance, a whispered prayer,
In hallowed moments, divinely rare.

A stitch of light in fabric torn,
In love's embrace, we are reborn.
Through laughter shared, and sorrows healed,
A timeless bond, forever sealed.

In golden rays of sunset's glow,
We gather close, our spirits flow.
With every pulse, a heartbeat's rhyme,
In hallowed moments, stitched in time.

Through every season, life's gentle change,
We find the strength that feels so strange.
In harmony, our souls entwine,
In sacred truth, our hearts align.

The Pathway of Yesterday's Blessings

In morning's glow, the light descends,
With prayers of peace, our spirit bends.
Each step we take, a gift bestowed,
In love's embrace, our hearts are sowed.

The past unfolds like petals fair,
Each memory, a whispered prayer.
Guided by stars, we walk anew,
With gratitude for all we do.

With faith as torch, we light the way,
Through trials faced, we kneel to pray.
The blessings drift like autumn leaves,
In every heart, a hope that weaves.

As night approaches, still we find,
The echoes of the love enshrined.
For every shadow holds a grace,
In every tear, a warm embrace.

So let us walk, hand in hand strong,
In the chorus of a timeless song.
The pathway glows with joy's own fire,
With every step, we rise, we aspire.

Whispers of Faith in Time's Embrace

In stillness deep, the whispers rise,
A gentle breath beneath the skies.
Where faith ignites, our spirits soar,
In time's embrace, we seek for more.

Each heartbeat sings of timeless grace,
In love's soft light, we find our place.
With tender hope, we journey near,
Through every doubt, we persevere.

In morning rays, the soul awakes,
With every dawn, a chance remakes.
A promise held in every tear,
In faith's bright glow, dispelling fear.

The pathways bend, yet lead us home,
In sacred trust, we freely roam.
Through trials faced, our hearts unite,
In whispered prayers, we find the light.

And when the dusk begins to fall,
Our hearts still hear the faithful call.
In every moment, love's embrace,
Whispers of faith, our saving grace.

Remnants of the Holy Path

Upon the path where shadows play,
The remnants of the saints convey.
Each step we tread, a story told,
In sacred echoes, pure and bold.

With every prayer, the heart ascends,
In love's embrace, the journey bends.
Through trials faced, we rise and fall,
In every whisper, hear the call.

The light of faith that guides our way,
Illuminates the darkest day.
With every breath, a chance renewed,
In harmony, our souls are hewed.

The holy ground beneath our feet,
Where spirit and the mortal meet.
With humble hearts, we seek to find,
The remnants of the love designed.

Through sacred grace, our spirits share,
The moments of a bright affair.
In every heart, a path to tread,
With kindness sown, our love is fed.

Seraphic Memories in Golden Light

In golden light, the memories shine,
With seraphic whispers, pure and divine.
Each moment cherished, a gift we see,
In love's embrace, we seek to be free.

The echoes of laughter, sweet as the morn,
In every heartbeat, a spirit reborn.
Through trials and joys, our paths entwine,
In every shadow, a spark will shine.

With faith as our anchor, the journey unfolds,
In golden moments, our truth beholds.
Each smile exchanged, a treasure shared,
In seraphic grace, we're always paired.

As twilight descends, the stars ignite,
With every memory, hearts take flight.
In the sacred silence, love resounds,
In every heartbeat, our peace abounds.

So let us bask in the soft retreat,
Where seraphic memories gently meet.
With every dawn, a promise bright,
In golden light, we find our right.

In the Presence of Angels and Memories

In the stillness of the night, we pray,
Whispers of angels guide our way.
With gentle hands, they lift our grief,
In their embrace, we find belief.

Memories dance like fleeting light,
Each moment cherished, pure and bright.
They weave the fabric of our soul,
In peace, our broken hearts feel whole.

Through trials faced, they stay near,
Anointed spirits, calm our fear.
Their harmonies in silence heard,
In every prayer, their grace conferred.

The path of love, we tread each day,
In faith, we walk, and hearts obey.
In every smile, in every tear,
The presence of angels, ever near.

The Spiritual Chronicles of Lives Lived

Beneath the stars, our stories flow,
Each life a thread, in light we grow.
Woven together by fate's design,
In each heartbeat, divinity shines.

Stories of strife and tales of grace,
Echo of love in this sacred space.
Through valleys deep, and mountains high,
Our spirits soar, as eagles fly.

With every tear and joyous song,
The chronicles reveal where we belong.
Eternal truths in hearts reside,
In the tapestry of time, we bide.

The wisdom of ages softly calls,
In every rise, in every fall.
The journey leads to wisdom's gate,
In the name of love, we navigate.

Echoes of Sacred Memory

In shadows cast by twilight's veil,
Echoes of memory start to sail.
Whispers of souls forever dear,
In sacred silence, they draw near.

Footsteps linger on hallowed ground,
In every corner, love is found.
The heart remembers all that's true,
In quiet moments, spirits renew.

As dawn breaks forth on the new day,
The past entwines in a gentle sway.
With every breath, we feel their grace,
In cherished whispers, we embrace.

Fragments of joy, and sorrow's sting,
In timeless dance, our souls take wing.
Each heartbeat a tale yet untold,
In echoes of memory, love unfolds.

Pilgrimage Through Time

With every step, we trace the light,
A pilgrimage through day and night.
Guided by faith, we journey on,
In the name of love, we are reborn.

Time flows gently, like a stream,
In every moment, we dare to dream.
Each lesson learned, a sacred gift,
In trials faced, our spirits lift.

From ancient paths to roads anew,
In sacred silence, we pursue.
The echoes of those who came before,
Guide our hearts to heaven's door.

In prayerful whispers, we unite,
A tapestry woven with purest light.
Through every season, through life's climb,
We seek the Divine on this journey through time.

Hymns of Yesteryear

In whispers soft, the ages call,
Their echoes dance through hallowed halls.
With voices raised, we sing in cheer,
To praise the love that draws us near.

Memories wrapped in golden light,
Illuminated through the night.
Each note a thread, a timeless bond,
With sacred hymns, our hearts respond.

In valleys deep, beneath the sky,
The stories live, they never die.
From every dawn, a promise made,
In faith and grace, we are remade.

Together we lift our hands and pray,
In joyous chorus, we find our way.
The past and present intertwined,
In love's warm glow, our souls aligned.

Forever cherished, never lost,
Through trials faced, we bear the cost.
Yet in the light of memories dear,
We find our hope, we draw them near.

Sacred memoria in Life's Mosaic

Each moment strung, a tapestry,
Of lives entwined, eternally.
In every thread, a story spun,
A sacred dance, all are as one.

Through valleys low and mountains high,
The sacred memory will never die.
In hearts of stone and hearts so free,
A vibrant hue of harmony.

The laughter shared, the tears we weep,
In every legacy, our dreams we keep.
With reverence, we hold the past,
In unity, our shadows cast.

Eternal peace, a guiding star,
In life's mosaic, near and far.
With every breath, a hymn we sing,
To honor the love that time will bring.

In sacred spaces, we unite,
With every candle, we ignite.
In gratitude, we lift our voice,
In faith, we make a sacred choice.

The Sanctuary of Sacred Remembering

In quietude, our spirits rise,
Within the sanctuary, wisdom lies.
Each sacred word, a guiding light,
To lead us through the darkest night.

We gather close, with open hearts,
Embracing love that never departs.
In every prayer, a warm embrace,
In every tear, we seek His grace.

The echoes of the saints resound,
In whispered prayers, we are found.
As candles burn, their flames unite,
A sacred bond, our hearts ignite.

In every story, we find our place,
In life's greatjourney, we seek embrace.
With gratitude, we take our stand,
In faith and love, we join His hand.

The sanctuary, a holy ground,
In every spirit, He is found.
As we remember, we shall see,
The beauty of eternity.

Divine Recollections and Their Light

In moments precious, time stands still,
With divine recollections that bless our will.
A light that guides through shadows cast,
Illuminating lessons from the past.

Each memory cherished, a sacred flame,
In whispers soft, we call His name.
With every heartbeat, prayers ascend,
In love's embrace, our souls transcend.

As seasons change, we gather near,
Collecting fragments held so dear.
In unity, our spirits soar,
With faith, we find forevermore.

The journey shared, the paths we trace,
In every moment, we see His face.
Transcending time, His light remains,
A guiding force through joys and pains.

In divine recollections, truth takes flight,
With open hearts, we seek His light.
Through every trial, we stand as one,
In love and grace, His will be done.

The Altar of Yesterday's Grace

In silent prayer, we bow our heads,
Remembering moments softly tread.
The altar shines with sacred light,
Illuminating wrongs made right.

In whispers lost, the past unfolds,
A tapestry of stories told.
Each thread a lesson, woven fine,
At yesterday's feet, our spirits entwine.

With hearts ablaze in gratitude,
We seek the peace of clemency's mood.
Forgiveness flows like gentle streams,
In grace, we rest and dream our dreams.

The echoes fade, yet memories stay,
Guiding us gently on our way.
For every sorrow, a joy shall rise,
In the altar's warmth, we find our ties.

A Journey Through the Cathedral of Time

Through arches high and shadows deep,
In sacred halls, our spirits leap.
The stained glass tells of yesteryears,
Each color drenched in joy and tears.

We wander paths of whispered prayers,
Where every moment holds love's layers.
The echoes chant a timeless hymn,
As hearts embrace the light within.

With every step, we seek the grace,
That leads us forth to a holy place.
Chasing visions of eternity,
In every breath, divinity.

The seasons change, yet still we find,
The ties that bless the heart and mind.
In this cathedral, we are whole,
A journey sealed in spirit's goal.

Memories Glorified in the Dawn

As dawn awakens, shadows flee,
Memories dance in light, so free.
Each moment wrapped in golden hue,
The past ignites what's fresh and new.

In morning's grace, the heart recalls,
The love within our sacred walls.
With every breath, the sunlight streams,
Awakening our sweetest dreams.

The whispers of the night decay,
As hope ascends to greet the day.
In tender warmth, our souls rejoice,
In dawn's embrace, we find our voice.

For every memory, a prayer we weave,
In gratitude, we shall believe.
Glorified in dawn's embrace,
We journey forth with love and grace.

Ethereal Insights from the Hills of Experience

From hills of wisdom, insights flow,
In every shadow, truth will grow.
With open hearts, we seek the night,
Finding meaning in the light.

The stars above, a cosmic guide,
Illuminating paths we bide.
In every step, a lesson clear,
From hills of time, we draw the near.

Through trials faced, our spirits rise,
With faith as strong as ancient ties.
In nature's arms, we find our peace,
Ethereal whispers that never cease.

In every storm, a leaf we glean,
For in the struggle, hearts careen.
Towards better days, we find our way,
With insights gained, we shall not sway.

Lost but Not Forgotten

In shadows deep, I came to roam,
A path unseen, away from home.
Yet in the night, a whisper came,
A gentle light, still calling my name.

Amidst the trials, I found my way,
A heart of faith, to guide the stray.
In every loss, a lesson learned,
Through sacred grief, my spirit burned.

Each tear I shed, a prayer in flight,
To seek the dawn from endless night.
Though lost I seemed, I'm never gone,
In every heart, my soul moves on.

The memories keep, a treasured hold,
In silent words, their truth unfolds.
I carry forth the love and grace,
In every breath, I find my place.

So even when the path is dim,
I stand with courage, hopes not slim.
For in the depths, I still believe,
That love once felt shall never leave.

The Lighthouses of My Journey

Through tempest's roar, I've sailed alone,
Yet guiding lights have brightly shone.
In storms of doubt, when shadows play,
I found my way, come what may.

Each lighthouse stands, a beacon true,
With arms stretched wide, to welcome you.
In every beam, a promise glows,
That hope remains, as spirit flows.

From rocky shores to distant seas,
I've journeyed far, on gentle breeze.
Each cherished soul a lantern bright,
Illuminating the dark of night.

No tempest fierce can dim the flame,
Nor waves of fear, bring grief or shame.
For in the hearts of those I meet,
I find the strength to stand on feet.

So let the winds of life be strong,
I carry forth this sacred song.
The lighthouses, my steadfast friends,
Guide me home, until journey ends.

In Communion with the Ages Past

In whispers soft, the ancients call,
Their voices echo through the hall.
With every turn of time's great wheel,
I sense the truths they long reveal.

In sacred texts, their wisdom lies,
A tapestry beneath the skies.
Each word a thread, each tale a guide,
In communion deep, the spirits bide.

From sacred fires to moonlit glades,
Their presence lingers, never fades.
As I reach out with heart and mind,
A bridge is built, our fates aligned.

In silent prayer, I honor they,
The sages' love shall light the way.
As time flows on, their lessons live,
In every breath, a gift we give.

So let my heart be open wide,
To learn in grace, with them abide.
In communion with the ages past,
Their timeless wisdom holds me fast.

The Garden of Past Lessons

In verdant lands where silence speaks,
A garden blooms, the soul it seeks.
Each flower tells a story grand,
Of trials faced and life's command.

The roots run deep in soil's embrace,
With every joy and every grace.
The petals soft, remind of pain,
In beauty's midst, the lessons gain.

With sunlight's kiss and rain's caress,
I gather strength from each distress.
In every season, growth appears,
Transforming grief into my tears.

So as I wander through this space,
I find the courage to embrace.
For every thorn that pricks my skin,
Has taught me how to bloom within.

Though storms may come to shake the ground,
In fervent faith, my roots are found.
In this garden, I shall remain,
A testament of love through pain.

Through the Lens of the Faithful Heart

In the silence, whispers rise,
The soul's gentle, hopeful sighs.
Faithful hearts seek the divine,
In each tear, His love we find.

Each prayer, a flower in bloom,
Chasing shadows, dispelling gloom.
With every breath, the spirit sings,
Of endless grace and holy things.

Guided by the sacred light,
Through the storm and darkest night.
Hands joined, we walk the sacred path,
Finding peace in holy wrath.

The vision grows, the heart expands,
Trusting in the Master's hands.
Though trials come and doubts may rise,
Faith endures, and never dies.

In every journey, love's embrace,
In humble prayer, we seek His face.
Through the lens of love we see,
All of life's sweet mystery.

The Labyrinth of Reminders

In the labyrinth, paths entwine,
Each turn a grace, each step a sign.
Echoes of wisdom softly call,
In shadows, light prepares to fall.

Every twist, a lesson learned,
Through the fire, our hearts are burned.
In wandering, we find our place,
In every heart, God's warm embrace.

The walls breathe stories of the past,
In stillness, find a truth that lasts.
Through trials faced, and kindness shown,
In the quiet, seeds are sown.

Puzzles woven through the night,
In the journey, hearts take flight.
A reminder of the paths we've tread,
In faith, we rise, in love we're led.

With each step, the spirit glows,
Through every turn, new hope bestows.
In the labyrinth, we discern,
The gentle call for hearts to learn.

Embracing the Echoes of Old

In the echoes of time gone by,
Whispers of faith dance in the sky.
Each lesson, a treasure to hold,
In the stories of the brave and bold.

Embrace the shadows of yesterday,
In the twilight, they softly play.
Memories, like stars, ignite,
Guiding the heart, a beacon of light.

Through ancient texts, we find our way,
In holy words, the truth will stay.
Gathered wisdom from those who've walked,
In stillness, their spirits have talked.

As seasons change, so must we grow,
In every heart, His love will flow.
Embrace the echoes, let them guide,
For in each moment, He abides.

With gratitude, we honor the past,
In faith, we tread, our souls steadfast.
Embracing the echoes, we become whole,
In the tapestry, His love consoles.

Graceful Reflections on the Road Behind

On the winding road of time,
Each step we take, a silent rhyme.
With every turn, we learn to see,
The grace that shapes our destiny.

Reflections dance like fading light,
In the darkness, hope ignites.
Through trials faced with faith renewed,
In every heart, His love accrued.

The past a mirror of our soul,
In every crack, the spirit whole.
Lessons carved in stone and sand,
By gentle hands, we understand.

With gratitude, we look behind,
In every sorrow, treasures find.
The road may twist, but love stays true,
Guiding us toward the light anew.

So here we stand, embracing time,
In the journey's grace, we find our rhyme.
Reflecting on where we have been,
In love's embrace, we rise again.

Memorials of the Heart's Path

In shadows cast by ancient trees,
A whisper calls, a gentle breeze.
Each step I take, a sacred vow,
To honor love, in this moment now.

The lanterns glow, their flicker bright,
Guiding me through the veil of night.
With every heartbeat, faith does swell,
In memory's embrace, I dwell.

The path is rough, yet beauty stays,
In trials faced, in endless praise.
Each tear a pearl, each loss a gain,
In sacred silence, I break my chain.

A tapestry of dreams unfolds,
In nature's arms, my spirit holds.
With every stone, a lesson learned,
In every fire, my heart has burned.

Together with the stars above,
I walk the trail, guided by love.
The past is stitched into my soul,
Each memorial makes me whole.

Reminders of the Sacred Journey

In stillness found within the heart,
A map unfolds, a sacred art.
With every breath, the journey calls,
In the quiet, the spirit sprawls.

Paths of wonder, trails of grace,
Through valleys low and high embrace.
The sacred whispers guide my way,
A gentle touch at break of day.

Every mountain climbed, each river crossed,
In every moment, I find the lost.
My faith, a compass, true and wise,
It leads me forth beneath the skies.

The echoes of the ancients sing,
In every season, hope takes wing.
With every sunrise, love reborn,
A promise wrapped in golden dawn.

Through prayers whispered on the breeze,
The universe grants me such ease.
Each reminder, a gift divine,
In every heartbeat, love shall shine.

Pilgrim's Reverie: The Journey Within

In the stillness of the mind,
A treasure trove I seek to find.
With every thought, a quiet quest,
To know the self, to find my rest.

Amidst the chaos, peace I glean,
From sacred whispers, soft and keen.
The heart, a compass, true and clear,
Guiding me through what I hold dear.

In dreams I wander, visions bright,
Through realms of shadow, into light.
Each step a prayer, each breath a verse,
In this pilgrimage, I might immerse.

The walls of doubt begin to fade,
As faith becomes the path I've made.
In the journey deep, I find my place,
In every heartbeat, a glimpse of grace.

In perfect stillness, truth unspools,
As wisdom flows, beyond the rules.
The soul's reflection, pure and kind,
A sacred journey, 'neath stars aligned.

Traces of Love in the Rearview

As I glance back on the road I've known,
Each footprint left, a seed that's sown.
In every twist, in every turn,
A flame of love forever burns.

In laughter shared, in sorrow we shared,
The bonds we formed, the ways we cared.
With each farewell, another bloom,
In memories wrapped, there's always room.

Reflecting now on all that's past,
The shadows fade, but love holds fast.
Through trials faced and joy embraced,
In every moment, hope is laced.

The road ahead may twist and wind,
Yet in my heart, your love I find.
The traces of you guide my slow stride,
Together still, though worlds divide.

In every sunrise, a flash of grace,
In every sunset, your sweet embrace.
These traces linger, a holy art,
Forever etched within my heart.

Chronicles Written in the Book of Life

In pages worn by prayer and grace,
Each story shared, a sacred trace.
The ink of faith, a river wide,
Leading souls where love abides.

Whispers of angels, gently stirred,
In every line, a holy word.
Through trials faced and shadows cast,
A testament of ages past.

With humble hearts, we seek the light,
To find our way through darkest night.
In every chapter, wisdom flows,
The seeds of joy, His mercy sows.

For every tear that stains the page,
A song of hope breaks free from cage.
Each moment lived, divine design,
In God's embrace, our hearts entwine.

The book unfolds, with promise bright,
In every word, a spark ignites.
With faith as compass, we shall steer,
Towards the love that draws us near.

Light Through the Veil of Time

In shadows deep, a beacon glows,
A gentle warmth that ever flows.
With hands uplifted, we arise,
To seek the truth beyond the skies.

The morning sun dispels the haze,
In radiance we sing His praise.
Through every trial, faith will shine,
An endless journey, love divine.

With eyes of hope, we look above,
To realms adorned with grace and love.
In every heartbeat, whispers call,
To rise and stand, to never fall.

The veil of time, so thin, so frail,
A sacred promise will prevail.
In every soul, His light ignites,
With every prayer, the heart ignites.

In twilight's glow, we find our way,
To anchor faith in each new day.
The Lord of life, forever near,
In every moment, He draws near.

The Sanctuary of Memories

In gentle whispers, memories reside,
A sacred space where hearts confide.
With every laugh and every tear,
The echoes of our souls are near.

Through seasons passed, the stories weave,
In threads of love, we come to believe.
Each moment etched, a timeless mark,
Illuminated by a holy spark.

In gratitude, we gather round,
To share the joy in what we've found.
Within this place of sacred grace,
The warmth of love we all embrace.

The light of faith, a guiding hand,
In every memory, we shall stand.
For in the heart, the stories flow,
A testament of love we know.

Together onward, we shall tread,
In past, present, the hope we spread.
The sanctuary, a gift divine,
In every heart, His love shall shine.

Timeless Echoes of Divine Wisdom

In silent prayer, the wisdom calls,
Through ancient texts, the knowledge falls.
Each truth revealed, a sacred light,
Guiding hearts through darkest night.

From ages past, the echoes sound,
In every soul, the truth is found.
With humble hearts, we strive to seek,
The joy and love that make us meek.

In every trial, His voice is clear,
A gentle nudge, forever near.
Timeless lessons we embrace,
In every challenge, we find grace.

With open minds and hearts aligned,
We walk the path, His light we find.
For every whisper, every sigh,
A chance to soar and lift on high.

The echoes ring, through time and space,
In every heartbeat, we find His grace.
With faith as refuge, we shall climb,
To reach the summit, so sublime.

Crossroads of Past and Present

At the crossroads where shadows dwell,
The footprints of time weave a tale.
Echoes of prayer, whispers of grace,
In every choice, a divine embrace.

Mountains stand tall, their roots in the dark,
While rivers flow on, igniting a spark.
Each moment a gift, held close to the heart,
With faith as our guide, we'll never depart.

The past holds lessons, both bitter and sweet,
While the present offers new paths to meet.
As dawn breaks anew, we gaze at the light,
Finding our way through the stillness of night.

In the silence we hear the sacred call,
A beckoning whisper, uniting us all.
With courage we stand, together we rise,
Embracing our journey, the truth never lies.

The Divine Memoir of a Surrendered Soul

Pages unfold with the ink of the past,
Each moment a prayer, a spell that is cast.
In surrender we find a refuge so pure,
A heart laid bare, eternally sure.

Through valleys of doubt, in shadows we tread,
Yet hope lights the path where the faithful have led.
With trust as our fortress, we weather each storm,
The love that surrounds us, forever keeps warm.

The memoir of grace, written in tears,
An ode to the journey that conquers our fears.
In every surrender, a miracle blooms,
A tapestry woven by love that consumes.

As clouds disperse and the sun breaks through,
We rise as a family, steadfast and true.
In unity's bond, we find our sweet role,
Embracing the essence of a surrendered soul.

Memories in the Light of Grace

Beneath the veil of a sacred night,
Memories dance in soft, gentle light.
Each flicker a heartbeat, a sigh from the past,
In the embrace of grace, our shadows are cast.

The laughter of angels fills the hallway of time,
Carrying echoes of love, pure and sublime.
In whispers of wisdom, our spirits align,
As fragments of glory begin to entwine.

We gather the moments like petals in hand,
Creating a garden, a divine wonderland.
In gratitude, we bow as the stars serenade,
Honoring the light in the choices we've made.

Each tear that has fallen, each joy we have penned,
Shapes the story of life, an eternal blend.
In the harvest of grace, we find peace anew,
A love that transcends, in every hue.

The Whispers of Yesterday's Truths

In the stillness of dusk, the past starts to speak,
Whispers of wisdom that echo so deep.
Memories woven like threads in the night,
Illuminate paths to the promise of light.

Each story tells of the battles we've faced,
In the forge of our souls, our lives have been laced.
With courage we walk on the shores of our fate,
Trusting the journey, no matter how late.

Beneath the old trees, their roots intertwine,
Lessons of love in each bend of the vine.
With reverence, we gather, the truths we once knew,
In the cradle of time, our spirits renew.

As dusk turns to dawn, and shadows retreat,
Yesterday's whispers guide us to meet.
In the tapestry woven with threads of the past,
We find tomorrow, our peace unsurpassed.

The Labyrinth of Graced Remembrance

In shadows deep, our steps we trace,
Through corridors of solemn grace.
With whispers soft, the past awakes,
Each memory a light that breaks.

In every turn, a lesson learned,
In quiet hearts, the fires burned.
We seek the path that leads us home,
In labyrinths of love, we roam.

With patience clad, we tread with care,
Through trials met, we rise from despair.
For in the steps, the Spirit guides,
Through every storm, His peace abides.

Our pilgrim souls, they weave the threads,
Of laughter, tears, and unsaid prayers.
In every heart, a song resides,
A chorus sung where faith abides.

And when we find the sacred door,
We'll dance with joy, forevermore.
A labyrinth of love divine,
In every twist, His light will shine.

Stones of Wisdom Along the Path of Faith

Each stone we place upon this way,
A testament to hope's bright sway.
With whispers kind, the ancients speak,
In every crack, the truth we seek.

Gathered here with hearts aglow,
In every stride, our spirits grow.
The wisdom found in silent night,
Guides weary souls towards the light.

Through rugged trails, the faithful tread,
With every tear, the spirit fed.
In trials faced, our strength reveals,
The sacred trust in how we heal.

Each stone a chapter, worn and wise,
Reflects the journey of the skies.
In faith's embrace, we stand as one,
Treading the path 'til labor's done.

For in the stones, the stories live,
Of love's great power to forgive.
With every step, we claim the grace,
Of wisdom found in faith's embrace.

Testimonies of the Soul's Sojourn

Each journey starts with faith in bloom,
Through deserts vast, or flowers' loom.
We wander forth, with hearts set free,
On trails of hope, in light we see.

In the quiet hours, voices call,
Echoes of love that break the fall.
Testimonies like lanterns bright,
Illuminate the darkest night.

Through valleys deep, our spirits soar,
In every step, we seek for more.
A tapestry of truth unfolds,
In stories shared, our faith beholds.

With every glance towards the skies,
Our gratitude to love's replies.
Through trials borne, the soul's pure song,
In every heart, where we belong.

For every sojourn, lessons learned,
In love's embrace, our flames have burned.
With every tear and every smile,
We walk this path, each sacred mile.

Celestial Breadcrumbs of Love and Forgiveness

Upon this path, we lightly tread,
With breadcrumbs left, where angels led.
In every heart, the grace does flow,
A journey marked by love bestowed.

Through trials faced, and moments shared,
We find the strength when others cared.
Forgiveness blooms in fertile ground,
In every loss, a grace profound.

Like stardust scattered in the night,
The echoes of our hearts take flight.
With gentle hands, we weave anew,
A tapestry of love so true.

From every pain, we rise and stand,
With open hearts, we join our hands.
For love unites and breaks the chains,
In every soul, forgiveness reigns.

So let us walk with lighted hearts,
Along the way where kindness starts.
With celestial crumbs, we share the grace,
Of love's embrace in every place.

Reflections of a Pilgrim's Heart

In shadows deep, I seek the light,
The path of truth, so pure and bright.
With every step, my spirit soars,
A journey bound for heaven's shores.

With prayerful hands, I lift my soul,
To find the peace that makes me whole.
Through trials faced, my faith will grow,
In pilgrim's heart, the love will flow.

The stars above, they guide my way,
In silent grace, I yearn to stay.
Each whispered promise, clear and true,
A testament to all I knew.

Through valleys low, and mountains high,
I navigate the endless sky.
For every tear, a lesson learned,
In faithful hearts, the fire's burned.

With every footstep, love's refrain,
A sacred song that calls my name.
To be a vessel, pure and kind,
A loving heart, forever aligned.

Divine Whispers of Yesteryear

In memories clad, the echoes ring,
Of gentle notes, the ages sing.
A tapestry of time unwinds,
In whispers soft, the heart it binds.

From ancient scrolls, the wisdom flows,
In timeless streams, the spirit grows.
Each prayerful thought, a treasure sought,
In every lesson, love is taught.

The light of faith that burns so bright,
Illuminates the darkest night.
In every shadow, hope appears,
To calm the storm, to dry our tears.

Through sacred texts, with reverence read,
We find the path, by angels led.
Each word, a seed of grace to sow,
In fields of peace, our spirits flow.

As seasons change, our hearts remain,
In silent prayer, we know no pain.
For divine whispers guide our way,
In yesterday's light, we find today.

The Gospel of Remembering

In silence shared, the stories weave,
Of days long lost, in hearts we cleave.
Each memory, a sacred breath,
A tale of life, a dance with death.

Through trials faced and joys embraced,
We carry wounds, yet love encased.
For every sorrow, grace restores,
The gospel speaks, forever pours.

In gatherings of the faithful few,
We share the strength in all we do.
With hands outstretched, we lift each other,
Remembering all, sister and brother.

Through songs of hope, our spirits rise,
In every heart, the truth belies.
For in remembrance, we find peace,
A steady stream that will not cease.

Each moment shared, a cherished gem,
In loving light, we honor them.
The gospel whispers through our years,
In joy, in faith, we dry our tears.

Threads of Faith Woven in Time

In woven threads, our lives entwined,
The fabric rich, the heart aligned.
With every stitch, a prayer is sewn,
In hopes and dreams, our seeds are grown.

From ancient looms, the stories told,
In every touch, the love unfolds.
A sacred bond that holds us tight,
In darkness deep, we seek the light.

Through trials faced, the fibers fray,
Yet strength remains to guide our way.
For every tear, a thread of grace,
In faith united, we find our place.

With grateful hearts, we lift our song,
In harmony where we belong.
Each note a thread, each chord a line,
In God's great tapestry, we shine.

As time flows on, the fabric grows,
In shared devotion, love bestows.
For threads of faith, forever spun,
In every heart, we are made one.

Devotional Scenes from Yesterday

In the quiet dawn, prayers rise,
Soft whispers join the morning light.
Reflecting on days of grace,
Each moment a sacred sight.

Through trials faced and tears shed,
Faith walked beside in every plight.
In the stillness, truth was said,
His love, my guiding light.

Old hymns echo in my soul,
Melodies that once were sung.
In their warmth, I feel made whole,
To Him, my heart is strung.

Beneath the oak, I used to pray,
Trusting in the unseen hands.
In the twilight's embrace, I stay,
Believing in His plans.

As the stars align up high,
They tell of journeys long and wide.
With every breath, I cannot lie,
In Him, my heart will abide.

Sanctified Echoes of My Journey

Wanderer's heart, drawn to the light,
Each step a prayer, each breath divine.
In shadows deep, faith shines bright,
In the dark, His love entwines.

Paths unknown, yet footsteps sure,
With grace as guide, I seek to know.
In every trial, love is pure,
From the seeds of faith, I grow.

Mountains high and valleys low,
Every summit bears His name.
In the stillness, rivers flow,
Whispers of hope, calling the same.

The echoes of yesterday's song,
Remind me of the way I tread.
In the harmony, I belong,
With every word of love I've spread.

Through sanctified moments shared,
The fabric of faith is sewn.
In unity, our hearts are paired,
In His grace, I have grown.

Beneath the Canopy of Grace

Beneath the vast and sheltering sky,
I find solace where spirits meet.
In the rustling leaves, a sigh,
Nature's hymn, gentle and sweet.

Every raindrop, a blessing falls,
With love woven in the air.
In the stillness, His voice calls,
In His arms, I am laid bare.

The sun breaks forth, a golden hue,
Painting hope across the land.
With each dawn, renewal true,
In His mercy, I firmly stand.

Through this journey, I have learned,
To seek His light in every strife.
In my heart, the flame has burned,
Guiding me through the dance of life.

Beneath the stars, I kneel in prayer,
Grateful for grace's embrace.
In each heartbeat, I declare,
Forever held in His embrace.

Remembrance at the Well of Faith

At the well where sorrows cease,
I gather thoughts, both old and new.
In the ripples, whispers of peace,
  Reflecting grace in every hue.

The water flows with stories deep,
Of broken paths and sweet redemption.
In every drop, the promises keep,
He holds my heart, my true intention.

Through trials faced like jagged stones,
Each lesson carved by faith's own hand.
In the silence, my spirit moans,
Yet rises, strong, to understand.

As I drink from this sacred place,
Renewed with hope, I find my way.
In His love, I find my grace,
  Guiding me in light of day.

I remember all that He has done,
For in my heart, His work is clear.
At the well of faith, I am one,
With every prayer, He draws near.

Illuminating the Darkness of Lost Years

In shadows deep, where hope seems lost,
We seek the light, regardless the cost.
Through trials faced and whispers heard,
We rise again, our spirits stirred.

The path may wane, the night seems long,
Yet faith ignites a vibrant song.
Each dawn unfolds a blessed chance,
To find our strength in purpose dance.

With every tear, a lesson blooms,
A light emerges through the glooms.
Through silent prayers and echoes vast,
We turn the page, embrace the past.

With hearts aglow, we walk in grace,
With every step, we find our place.
Though years may fade, our spirits soar,
In love's embrace, we seek for more.

So let the light of ages shine,
Transform the dark, and intertwine.
For in each moment, wisdom's near,
Illuminating all our fear.

Spirit's Guiding Stars Through Time

Throughout the ages, stars align,
Guiding our hearts, a sacred sign.
In vast expanse, they shine so bright,
Illuminating paths of light.

Each twinkle whispers secrets true,
As journeys weave, both old and new.
With every guide, a purpose found,
In spirit's touch, we're tightly bound.

Through darkest nights, when hope seems frail,
The stars above tell sacred tales.
They dance and shimmer, dreams ignite,
In faith we find our sacred sight.

So raise your eyes to heavens wide,
Let spirit's stars be our guide.
For in their light, our souls will soar,
In unity, forevermore.

With hearts aligned, we chase the dawn,
The guiding stars, we carry on.
Through love and light, we shall ascend,
In spirit's glow, the journey blends.

The Sacred Archive of Memories

In quiet halls where echoes dwell,
The memories share their fragile spell.
Each fleeting thought, a treasure rare,
In love's embrace, we lay it bare.

The gentle whispers of times gone by,
Remind us how the spirit flies.
In every laugh, in every tear,
The sacred archive holds us near.

With reverent hearts, we turn the pages,
Of life's great book through all the stages.
Each story told, a glimpse of grace,
In every corner, love's warm face.

The past we honor, the future calls,
With every chapter, wisdom falls.
In memory's light, we find our peace,
And in its depth, our souls release.

So cherish well the sacred page,
In every line, the fleeting age.
For in the heart, the archives gleam,
A tapestry of truth and dream.

Chronicles Written in Faith's Light

In ancient scrolls, the stories dwell,
Of faith that conquers, love's bright swell.
Through trials faced, through battles won,
The chronicles of life begun.

With ink of hope, the truth laid bare,
Each line a promise, woven with care.
Through darkest nights and harshest days,
In faith's embrace, we seek the ways.

The wisdom shared, the lessons learned,
In every heart, the passion burned.
As scribes of life, our tales unfold,
In shimmering light, the stories told.

The whispers echo from ages past,
In faith's embrace, we find our cast.
With every word, a destiny shaped,
In love's pure glow, our fears escaped.

So let us write with fervent heart,
The chronicles that never part.
For in each line, our spirits rise,
In faith's light, we touch the skies.

The Light Beyond the Seasons

In dawn's embrace, the promise shines,
A whisper soft, divine designs.
Through winter's chill and summer's blaze,
We find our strength in holy ways.

The night will yield to morning's grace,
Each season flows in sacred space.
With every leaf that falls and grows,
God's love in nature ever shows.

In storms that rage and calm that falls,
We hear the echo of His calls.
The light will guide through darkest fears,
A beacon bright through all the years.

When springtime blooms, our hearts renew,
In fields of gold, our faith will strew.
The light beyond, forever beams,
A tapestry of hope and dreams.

So let us walk in sacred light,
Embrace the day, rejoice the night.
For in each season, near and far,
We find the bloom in every star.

Testimonies of Trials and Triumphs

In valleys low, our spirits bend,
Yet faith will rise, our heart's defend.
For every tear that leaves a trace,
God holds us close in warm embrace.

Through fire's trial, we forge anew,
A testimony built on true.
In darkest nights, His voice will guide,
Through every storm, we will abide.

Though mountains loom, we stand as one,
With hope and love, the battle's won.
Our scars, a mark of victories found,
In every struggle, grace abounds.

From ashes rise, like phoenix bright,
The heart restored, the spirit's flight.
In trials faced, our strength will show,
In every pain, God's mercy flows.

Together we will share our song,
In faith and love, we all belong.
Testimonies echo true and loud,
In every heart, the love is proud.

Visions from the Hallowed Ground

In silence deep, the whispers come,
A sacred call, the heart's own drum.
From hallowed ground, we seek the view,
In every breath, the old made new.

As shadows dance in twilight's gleam,
We catch the eye of heaven's dream.
The ancient stones bear witness bold,
To stories sown, both young and old.

With every step, the echoes sing,
In harmony, our praises ring.
A vision bright, from past to grace,
In love's embrace, we find our place.

Communion sweet, in spirits twined,
We seek His face, with hearts aligned.
On hallowed ground, the faithful tread,
With every prayer, the spirit fed.

The light that shines, forever flows,
In visions shared, the heartware grows.
From hallowed ground, our hopes arise,
In every soul, the promise lies.

The Altar of Reflection

Upon the altar, thoughts entwined,
In quietude, our souls aligned.
Each moment past, a sacred gift,
In stillness here, our spirits lift.

With grateful hearts, we pause to see,
The lessons learned, the path to be.
In every trial, a chance to grow,
The seeds of faith in us will sow.

As candles flicker, memories glow,
We find the grace in ebb and flow.
In prayers lifted, our hopes abide,
The altar holds what hearts confide.

In every tear, a promise clear,
In every joy, the light draws near.
Each thought a prayer, each sigh a hymn,
The altar whispers, "You are Him."

So come, reflect, and find your peace,
In sacred space, our fears release.
The altar stands, a holy place,
In every heart, we seek His grace.

Echoes of the Heart's Journey

Upon the path where shadows cease,
The whispers call, they bring us peace.
With every step, the heart does yearn,
In sacred light, our souls discern.

Through valleys low and mountains high,
We seek the truth beneath the sky.
In trials faced, our spirits rise,
United then, in love we prize.

Each moment shared, a gift divine,
In fellowship, our hopes align.
For in the journey, bonds are made,
In holy echo, never fade.

The heart's journey, a winding thread,
With faith as light, where angels tread.
Every lesson, a sacred guide,
In every sorrow, love abides.

So let us walk this road in grace,
With open hearts, we seek Your face.
For in each echo, we are known,
In love's embrace, we are not alone.

Reflections in the Still Waters

In mirrors calm, the heavens gleam,
The stillness speaks, a tranquil dream.
With every ripple, stories flow,
Of faith and love, we come to know.

Beneath the surface, depth untold,
In quiet moments, hearts unfold.
A sacred peace, in silence found,
With every breath, we are unbound.

The waters speak of grace and truth,
In youth's bright glow and wisdom's tooth.
Reflecting light, our spirits soar,
In stillness dwells the evermore.

By waters clear, we lay our cares,
In sacred space, our hearts lays bare.
With gentle waves, we leave behind,
The burdens borne, our souls unwind.

So let us gaze, with hearts laid bare,
In still waters, find solace rare.
For in the calm, His love invites,
Reflected grace, our guiding lights.

Divine Footprints on Sacred Soil

In every step upon this ground,
The footprints of our Lord are found.
With every heartbeat, grace bestowed,
In sacred soil, our faith has grown.

The earth does speak of stories near,
Of love's embrace and quiet cheer.
Through trials faced, His hand we feel,
With every wound, our hearts to heal.

Each footprint marks a path of light,
In darkest days, it shines so bright.
Through storm and strife, we find our way,
In faith's strong grip, we learn to pray.

As footsteps echo through the years,
In joy and sorrow, hopes and fears.
In all we walk, we find Him there,
In sacred soil, His love laid bare.

So let us tread with hearts aflame,
In every footstep, praise His name.
For in the journey, truth unveils,
Divine footprints, love prevails.

Chronicles of Grace from Days Gone By

In whispered tales of days gone by,
Echoes of grace in every sigh.
From trials faced to joys embraced,
The chronicles of love, interlaced.

With timeless wisdom, hearts grow bold,
In stories shared, the truth unfolds.
Through valleys deep and mountains grand,
In every chapter, a guiding hand.

The past, a canvas richly drawn,
In every stroke, the hope of dawn.
From sorrow's grip to joyful tunes,
In grace, our spirits find maroons.

So gather 'round, let history sing,
Of moments blessed, of joy we bring.
In every memory, light shall shine,
A sacred legacy, pure and fine.

With every heartbeat, learn from yore,
In chronicles of grace, we explore.
Through faith in past, our futures rise,
In love eternal, our hope lies.

The Sacred Archive of Human Experience

In quiet folds, the stories lie,
A tapestry of souls who sigh.
Each moment captured in grace's flow,
The sacred dance of ebb and glow.

In every heart, a truth concealed,
A whisper soft, the spirit healed.
The lessons learned, the trials faced,
In every tear, a love embraced.

Journey forth through ancient lands,
Where wisdom rests in gentle hands.
The sacred archive should be sought,
In every breath, the battles fought.

With reverent gaze, the past we trace,
In shadows linger light's embrace.
The stories weave through time's vast sphere,
An echo found in joy and fear.

In every heart, a flame ignites,
Guide us, O creation's lights.
Through trials, triumphs, love, and pain,
We find our truth, through joy and strain.

Echoes of the Divine in Every Step

Upon the path where angels tread,
The whispers of the sacred spread.
Each footfall speaks of grace and peace,
In every stride, a sweet release.

In morning dew and evening's sigh,
The soul awakens, lifts to fly.
The echoes ring in hearts so true,
A symphony of all we've due.

With every heartbeat, love's refrain,
We dance through joy and weather pain.
The sacred guide in shadows cast,
An inner light, forever vast.

The universe sings a holy song,
In every moment, we belong.
Divine reflections in stillness found,
In the silence, grace unbound.

So let us walk, hand in hand,
With hearts aglow, on sacred land.
For in each step, we find our prayer,
Divine echoes linger everywhere.

A Reverent Glance at the Hallowed Past

In hallowed halls where whispers dwell,
The stories of the ages swell.
With reverent gaze, we turn the page,
To honor those who walked this stage.

The trials faced, the battles won,
In every struggle, light was spun.
They forged a path, though dark the night,
To guide us towards the day's first light.

Cloaked in wisdom, their voices call,
In echoes sweet, they rise and fall.
A lineage of love now flows,
In the seeds of truth, the spirit grows.

Let us remember each sacred thread,
For in their dreams, our hearts are fed.
With humbled hearts, we cast our gaze,
Upon the past, we sing their praise.

The sacred ties that bind us here,
With every heartbeat, loud and clear.
Through time's embrace, we find our place,
A reverent glance at boundless grace.

Chronicles of Light Amidst Shadows

In shadows cast where doubts may creep,
The light emerges, secrets keep.
Chronicles of hope alive,
In every soul, the spark shall thrive.

Through trials deep, a flame ignites,
Guiding hearts to reach new heights.
Within the dark, a truth shines bright,
In every breath, we seek the light.

With every moment, courage swells,
As whispers turn to ringing bells.
In shadows, lessons softly bloom,
As strength ascends to chase the gloom.

Together we rise, hand in hand,
Through every storm, we make our stand.
Chronicles weave a tapestry,
In the shadowed night, we choose to see.

For in our hearts, the radiance beams,
Illuminating hope and dreams.
Light amidst the shadows flows,
In love eternal, life bestows.

The Covenant of Remembering

In stillness we gather, hearts in refrain,
To honor the promise, our souls' sweet chain.
Remember the whispers of ages gone by,
In the silence, His presence, we cannot deny.

With each breath we take, we weave sacred bonds,
Fulfilling the pact that forever responds.
Together we stand, in faith we unite,
In the warmth of His grace, we find our light.

Through trials and storms, in shadows we tread,
Yet lifted by love, we rise from the dread.
The Covenant strong, it binds us just so,
In remembering Him, we learn how to grow.

As seasons keep turning, our memories flow,
In the garden of time, His blessings we sow.
Let the echoes remind us of what must be known,
In the heart's quiet chamber, we are never alone.

So hold dear the moments, each promise we make,
In the tapestry woven, the threads never break.
The Covenant endures, our spirits entwined,
In the light of His mercy, our hope is enshrined.

In the Shadow of the Divine

Beneath the vast heavens, a whisper so clear,
We dwell in the warmth of the love that we hear.
In shadows of grace, our spirits reside,
In the presence of mercy, we seek and abide.

Each morning unfolds with a promise so bright,
Guided by faith, we embrace the light.
In the shadow of glory, our burdens set free,
With hands open wide, we kneel on our knees.

Through valleys of sorrow, we walk side by side,
In the knowing of Him, our fears will subside.
The journey is sacred, each step a prayer,
In the shadow of love, we find solace there.

And when the night falls, in silence we glow,
Trusting the path that the heart longs to know.
In the stillness, we gather, our voices as one,
In the shadow of the Divine, our fears come undone.

So let not your spirit be heavy with care,
For the shadow holds blessings, in moments we share.
Embrace the connection, the light will align,
In the arms of the faith, we forever entwine.

Celestial Ink on Life's Scroll

With each dawn that breaks, a page freshly turned,
The ink of the heavens, through trials we've learned.
On the scroll of existence, our stories unfold,
In celestial whispers, His truths are retold.

The tapestry woven, in colors divine,
Holds the echoes of ages, where our spirits entwine.
Each word, a reflection of grace deep within,
In the light of His love, we find where we've been.

In moments of stillness, the heart can discern,
The lessons of patience, the wisdom we earn.
Celestial ink flows, as we carve out our fate,
In the dance of creation, the love we await.

Through valleys and mountains, the journey is grand,
With faith as our compass, together we stand.
In the richness of life, His presence we trace,
On the scroll that we cherish, we find our own place.

So let us write boldly, with passion and zeal,
For the story of life is a wondrous reveal.
Celestial ink guides us, in love we enroll,
Together forever, on life's precious scroll.

The Testament of Memory's Light

In the heart of remembrance, a candle does glow,
Illuminating paths where the faithful shall go.
A testament holds what our spirits once knew,
In the tapestry woven, His love shines right through.

Each memory cherished is a treasure so dear,
A beacon of hope, dispelling our fear.
With whispers of wisdom, we gather as one,
In the testament's embrace, our journey's begun.

Through moments of joy and tears that have fell,
We find strength in the stories that our hearts tell.
For the light of our memories ignites the new day,
In the testament's truth, we find our own way.

As seasons keep shifting, the past finds its grace,
In the light of our memories, His love we embrace.
We walk hand in hand, through the shadows we stride,
In the testament of love, forever our guide.

So treasure the moments, let the stories unfold,
For the testament of memory is a tale to be told.
In the light of His mercy, our spirits ignite,
In the journey of faith, we bask in His light.

Reverent Remembrance of the Past

In quiet halls of yesteryears,
We gather echoes of our tears.
Voices whisper, soft and low,
Guiding us where memories flow.

With every prayer, a light ignites,
Illuminating sacred sights.
We honor paths we've walked before,
On ancient trails, forevermore.

Each laughter shared, each tear we shed,
A tapestry of love, well spread.
In reverence, we pause and see,
The grace that shaped our history.

In stillness, heartbeats softly chime,
Echoing the pulse of time.
A journey carved in faith's embrace,
A sacred song, our past's grace.

Let our souls find peace and rest,
In memories, forever blessed.
For all we've lost and all we've gained,
In reverent love, our hearts retained.

The Sacred Tapestry of Days Gone By

Threads of twilight weave our past,
In sacred pattern, forever cast.
Moments stitched with love and care,
A timeless tale, we gladly wear.

Each thread a thought, each hue a sigh,
Casting shadows that never die.
We journey forth with heart and soul,
In the tapestry, we find our whole.

From dawn's first light to evening's grace,
We find the sacred in every space.
A tapestry of joy and pain,
Binding us together in joy's refrain.

In every stitch, a lesson learned,
In every color, a candle burned.
History whispers through the ages,
Awakening hope on fragile pages.

Let us cherish each thread that binds,
For in our hearts, true legacy finds.
A sacred web of days gone by,
With gratitude we reach for the sky.

Miracles in Reminiscence

In the quietude of memory's grace,
We witness miracles time can't erase.
Each moment a blessing, pure and bright,
Illuminated by love's gentle light.

When shadows loom, and doubts arise,
Recall the wonders that fill our skies.
For every tear that fell like rain,
A rainbow forms from joy and pain.

Through every trial we have embraced,
Miracles flourish, hope interlaced.
In humble hearts, faith's seeds are sown,
In reminiscence, we rise, we've grown.

With every step on this sacred path,
We find redemption in our aftermath.
Echoes of grace, so sweetly played,
In gentle whispers, love won't fade.

In gratitude, we lift our voice,
In remembrance, we rejoice.
For miracles dwell in histories spun,
Evermore under the same sun.

Recalling the Blessings of Old

In the stillness of twilight's glow,
We gather blessings from long ago.
With thankful hearts, we lift our eyes,
Embracing truth beyond the skies.

Each memory a gift, softly shared,
A tapestry of love, thoroughly cared.
Through trials faced and joys revealed,
In faith, our hearts are gently healed.

Let us remember laughter's sound,
In every moment, grace we found.
Each whispered prayer, a sacred bond,
With every heartbeat, we respond.

Amidst the storms that life may bring,
We find the song our spirits sing.
For in the past, a light remains,
A guiding star through joys and pains.

So let us cherish blessings bestowed,
In the sacred light, our path is showed.
For every memory held so dear,
Recalls the love that draws us near.

Reverberations of a Faithful Journey

In shadows deep, we seek the light,
With whispered prayers, hearts take flight.
Every step, a testament of grace,
Guided by faith, in this sacred space.

Through trials faced, we rise anew,
With each heartbeat, love shines through.
In unity, we carry on,
A chorus sweet, a faithful song.

Oft' we stumble, often we stray,
Yet hope remains, a bright array.
In every tear, a lesson learned,
In every joy, our spirits burned.

Hand in hand, we journey far,
Light of the world, our guiding star.
With open hearts, and eyes that see,
The sacred path unfolds with glee.

Together we rise, our voices strong,
In harmony, we all belong.
For every journey, a sacred thread,
In reverberations, our truth is spread.

From the Depths of the Soul

In silence deep, the spirit speaks,
From hidden depths, the heart then seeks.
A journey inward, void of fear,
For in the dark, the light draws near.

Through valleys low, and mountains high,
We navigate with faith, not sigh.
Each whisper soft, a gentle guide,
Through storms of life, we shall abide.

In every sorrow, in every cheer,
A sacred bond that draws us near.
In every shadow, the grace shines bright,
Illumined paths lead us to light.

The soul's caress, a sweet embrace,
In tender moments, we find grace.
To those who wander, lost in pain,
Know that love will break the chain.

From depths we rise, connected whole,
In every heartbeat, we find goal.
Together bound, the journey long,
In depths of soul, our hearts belong.

Ephemeral Grace: The Past Seen Clearly

In fleeting time, we glimpse the past,
Each moment carved, each memory cast.
With clarity gained through trials' sway,
We find our footing, come what may.

The echoes linger of lessons learned,
In gentle waves, our spirits turned.
For every shadow, a light remains,
In fleeting grace, our truth sustains.

The past a canvas, painted bold,
In every hue, our stories told.
With open hearts, we face the dawn,
In ephemeral grace, life is drawn.

Wisdom whispers in whispers soft,
In moments cherished, spirits loft.
To see the beauty in every scar,
Transforms the journey, near and far.

So hold the past, let it guide,
In every step, with arms open wide.
For in this grace, we truly see,
The threads of life in unity.

Divine Patterns in Life's Weaving

In every thread, a story spun,
A tapestry, where we're all one.
With colors bright, and shadows too,
Life's weaving speaks of love so true.

Each pattern formed, a sacred art,
With every loop, we play our part.
Together crafted, in divine dance,
Embracing fate, we take the chance.

In weaving paths, we find our way,
With every moment, we learn to stay.
Through laughter sweet and sorrow's sigh,
We find connection, you and I.

The loom of life, both fierce and kind,
In threads of hope, our souls entwined.
With faith as guide, we boldly tread,
In life's great weave, no words unsaid.

The patterns shift, the stories share,
In every heart, divine care.
So let us weave, with love in hand,
A magnificent, united strand.

For every life, a sacred thread,
In divine patterns, we are led.
To trust the weave, and dance along,
In life's rich fabric, we belong.

A Chronicle of Sacred Footsteps

In the meadow where shadows play,
Each step echoes a hymn of old.
Guided by stars that softly sway,
A tale of love in silence told.

Through valleys deep where rivers flow,
Whispers of spirits in the breeze.
Each heartbeat marks a sacred glow,
Unlocking paths with gentle ease.

The mountains rise with ancient grace,
Carving stories in the dust.
The sun alights on every face,
A bond of faith, a holy trust.

With every dawn, new hope is born,
Woven in tapestries of light.
Awake the soul, no longer worn,
Finding solace in the night.

In these sacred steps, we tread,
A journey fueled by grace divine.
Our hearts entwined, we forge ahead,
In love's embrace, forever shine.

Faithful Records in Time's Embrace

In the book of life, the pages turn,
Each word a prayer softly spoken.
With every lesson, the heart can learn,
A vow of love that shall not be broken.

The clock ticks on with rhythmic grace,
Marking moments of sacred trust.
In the silence, we find our place,
Among the letters of dust to dust.

As seasons change, the spirit grows,
Every sorrow, a thread of gold.
Through joy and pain, true beauty shows,
The legacy of love retold.

In twilight hours, we gather near,
Sharing tales of those who came.
With laughter ringing, love draws near,
A faithful heart ignites the flame.

So, let us write with courage bold,
The records of our days divine.
In time's embrace, our stories told,
A tapestry of love we twine.

With Each Beat, I Remember

With each beat, I feel the call,
A rhythm of faith that guides my way.
The sacred echoes never fall,
A melody that won't decay.

In the stillness of a quiet night,
The heart recalls its primal song.
Awash in grace, the soul takes flight,
In the embrace where we belong.

The whispers of ages past resound,
Each pulse a story yet to share.
In every heartbeat, love is found,
A treasure kept with utmost care.

Through trials faced and mountains moved,
The spirit breathes in every sigh.
With each beat, the past is proved,
A legacy that will not die.

So linger here, oh cherished friend,
With every beat, we walk as one.
In faith we trust, and love transcend,
Together 'neath the rising sun.

Heartbeats of a Forgotten Time

Heartbeats echo through the years,
In the stillness, the past awakes.
Each thump a whisper, laced with tears,
A journey woven in love's stakes.

Through candlelight and shadows cast,
The sacred moments softly gleam.
In each heartbeat, memories last,
A thread of hope, a timeless dream.

Faces fade, yet hearts remain,
Carried high on wings of grace.
Through every joy and every pain,
Love's reflection lights the space.

In prayerful reverence, we stand,
United in this sacred rhyme.
Our souls uplifted, hand in hand,
We honor heartbeats lost in time.

So listen close, the echoes call,
In every heartbeat, love's embrace.
Through sacred paths, we rise and fall,
In memories, we find our place.

Holy Shadows of My Path

In the quiet of the night, I pray,
Guided by light in disarray.
Holy shadows softly call,
Whispering truths to one and all.

Angels watch with tender grace,
Illuminating each misplaced trace.
In faith, I walk through trials and fears,
Finding solace beyond my tears.

Each step reveals a hidden sign,
A promise etched in the divine.
Through valleys low and mountains tall,
I find Your love surrounding all.

With every breeze, Your spirit flows,
In sacred moments, our bond grows.
I seek the way, though shadows fall,
In Your embrace, I stand tall.

You lead me on this hallowed quest,
In every heart, You find a nest.
Holy shadows guide me true,
In every breath, I long for You.

Remnants of Grace: A Journey

Upon this path where grace fell down,
I gather remnants, not a crown.
With every footstep marked by pain,
My soul sings softly, free from disdain.

The road winds on through thick and thin,
Where storms may rage, but love begins.
In remembrance of the sacred ties,
I breathe the depths of ancient skies.

Each lesson learned, a gem refined,
In trials faced, Your light I find.
With every tear and joyful glance,
I rise anew, in hope, I dance.

The journey leads through darkest nights,
Yet in the shadows, Your love ignites.
With faith as guide and heart ablaze,
I walk in peace, in endless praise.

Remnants of grace, we weave our fate,
In unity, we stand, not late.
For in this journey, endless and vast,
Your love, O Lord, will ever last.

Chronicles of the Soul's Recollection

In the stillness of a mindful hour,
I pen the tales of grace and power.
Each memory, a sacred thread,
Woven where the spirit has led.

Whispers echo from days of old,
Stories of mercy waiting to be told.
In the chambers of my soul's embrace,
I find the warmth of Your holy space.

Pages turn in the softest light,
As dawn breaks forth, banishing night.
Each line a prayer, each word a plea,
In the chronicles, I come to see.

The sacred dance of joy and strife,
In every trial, I glimpse eternal life.
Memory's embrace, a gentle guide,
Uniting hearts in love and pride.

Chronicles written in ink divine,
A testament of grace entwined.
In every heart, Your stories bloom,
In this journey, we find our room.

Celestial Footprints in the Dust

Amidst the earth, where shadows lie,
I seek the stars in the vast sky.
Celestial footprints mark my way,
Guiding my heart to where You stay.

In every grain, a world unfolds,
Stories of love and faith retold.
With every step, I feel Your grace,
In these fleeting moments, I find my place.

The silence speaks; the winds agree,
Nature's hymn, a symphony.
In the dance of dawn's soft hue,
I find the beauty that comes from You.

With every heartbeat, whispers roam,
Calling me back to my true home.
Celestial echoes through the dust,
In every soul, You still, I trust.

I follow footprints on this trail,
With joyous spirit that will not fail.
In heavenly realms where love abides,
I walk the path with You as guide.

Reverberations of the Sacred Quest

In shadows deep, where whispers dwell,
The soul embarks, it's time to tell.
Guided by lights of heavens above,
The path unfolds, a journey of love.

With every tear, a lesson learned,
In quiet prayers, the heart is turned.
Mountains rise and valleys fall,
Yet faith endures, through it all.

In stillness found, the answers bloom,
A sacred dance dispels the gloom.
As stars alight the night's embrace,
We find our truth, we seek His grace.

Through trials faced, our spirits soar,
In every breath, we yearn for more.
The sacred quest, both near and far,
Awakens hope, our guiding star.

So let us walk, hand in hand,
In love and faith, together we stand.
The echoes of this journey will last,
As we embrace the future and past.

Testaments of Love in Life's Canvas

With gentle strokes, the heart paints true,
A tapestry rich, in every hue.
Moments cherished, forever bleed,
In vibrant dreams, our spirits feed.

Each whisper shared, a bond we weave,
In love's embrace, we choose to believe.
Through storms we sail, through calm we glide,
Testaments of love, our endless pride.

The canvas wide, our stories blend,
In every heart, a message sends.
With laughter bright and tears that flow,
Life's masterpiece begins to glow.

So paint with grace, let colors burst,
In every heartbeat, quench your thirst.
For love transcends, it knows no bounds,
In life's great canvas, joy resounds.

Together we'll sketch the days ahead,
In sacred lines, no words unsaid.
Through every shade, our passions flare,
Testaments of love beyond compare.

Seeds of Hope Planted in the Past

In fertile grounds where dreams take root,
Seeds of hope, fragile yet astute.
Nurtured by faith, they strive to rise,
Reaching towards the endless skies.

Through seasons dark, they brave the storm,
In every crack, they seek the warm.
Burdened hearts can find release,
In tiny sprouts, a bloom of peace.

Remember the moments, tender and rare,
Each seed a memory, handled with care.
With patience grown, and love as light,
The past reveals its beauty bright.

For in the soil of yesterday,
Lie hidden gems that gently sway.
Hope's gentle nudge guides us along,
In the dance of life, we find our song.

So tend to the garden, let it thrive,
With every heartbeat, come alive.
In the bounty of love, our spirits soar,
Seeds of hope, forever more.

The Celestial Melody of Yesteryears

In twilight's glow, the stars align,
A melody soft, a sacred sign.
Echoes of laughter, whispers of dreams,
In the heart's chamber, magic redeems.

The past resounds, a symphony sweet,
In every heartbeat, time's gentle beat.
Weaving the moments, the joys and fears,
A celestial song echoes through years.

With every note, a story unfolds,
Traditions cherished, and memories bold.
Harmonies blend, like rivers that flow,
The melody rich, as spirits glow.

As sunsets fade, the dawn shall rise,
In every shadow, the light will prize.
The celestial dance, forever near,
A song of hope that draws us here.

So listen closely, to the whispers of time,
In the rhythm of life, our hearts will climb.
For yesteryears cradle our sacred grace,
In the celestial melody, we find our place.

Eternal Embrace of My Spiritual Heritage

In the stillness of the night,
Whispers of ages past sing,
Guiding my soul through shadows,
Embracing the light they bring.

Roots entwined in sacred ground,
Awakening echoes of grace,
I walk the path they once trod,
United in love's warm embrace.

A tapestry woven with faith,
Threads of devotion and lore,
Binding my heart to their strength,
A heritage I can't ignore.

In prayers lifted to the skies,
Voices of ancestors soar,
Their blessings a gentle tide,
Guiding me forevermore.

In this eternal embrace,
I find solace, I find peace,
A journey of love transcends,
In heritage, my soul's release.

The Quiet Grace of Retrospection

In silent moments I reflect,
On the paths my feet have traced,
Gentle whispers of the past,
In memories, I find grace.

Each shadowed corner holds a prayer,
A lesson wrapped in time's embrace,
I gather strength from stories lived,
Finding hope in their trace.

The heart recalls both joy and strife,
In sacred stillness, I explore,
With gratitude, I hold each breath,
The quiet grace that I restore.

Through trials faced, my spirit grew,
Each stumble shaped my soul's design,
In retrospection, I find peace,
With love's thread, my heart aligns.

As I ponder life's vast expanse,
I see the light that guides my way,
In quiet grace, I take my stand,
Cherishing each fleeting day.

Ancestral Prayers in the Echoes

Echoes of prayers drift and weave,
Through valleys deep and mountains high,
Ancestral voices whisper soft,
In the stillness, they reply.

They beckon me to honor roots,
To stand firm in sacred trust,
For each heartbeat carries tales,
In faith's embrace, I feel robust.

With every dawn, their dreams arise,
Cradled in the warmth of light,
I am the vessel of their hopes,
In the darkness, I reignite.

Their prayers echo through my heart,
A symphony of love divine,
Unraveling the threads of time,
In this sacred tapestry, I shine.

As night descends, I find my peace,
In the whispers of the past,
Ancestral prayers guide my way,
In their embrace, I'm home at last.

Pilgrims of the Heart: Reflections

We are pilgrims on this earth,
Seeking truth with every stride,
With hearts ablaze, we wander forth,
In love's embrace, we abide.

Every step, a sacred dance,
In nature's grace, we find our song,
Tracing trails of ancient faith,
Reminding us that we belong.

Reflections of the stars above,
Guide us through the night's deep hour,
In moments still, we hear the call,
To awaken love's fierce power.

With each breath drawn from the earth,
We hold the echoes of the wise,
In unity, our spirits soar,
Together, we transcend the skies.

As pilgrims of the heart, we seek,
In every soul, a sacred fire,
To journey on, hand in hand,
Fulfilling our truest desire.

Pearls of Wisdom from the Past

In days of yore, the ancients spoke,
Their words like stars, a guiding cloak.
Through trials faced and burdens borne,
Their wisdom shines, a light reborn.

With each tale shared, a lesson learned,
In sacred scrolls, our hearts are turned.
To cherish dreams, and heed the call,
To rise from ashes, above the fall.

In every struggle, faith does grow,
A river deep, where spirits flow.
For in the quiet, God's voice we hear,
In moments lost, His path draws near.

Reverent echoes from ages past,
Our souls entwined, in shadows cast.
These pearls of wisdom, treasures rare,
A holy gift, beyond compare.

So ponder well the tales they weave,
In every heart, a chance to believe.
Through lineage strong, we seek what's true,
And find our place in skies of blue.

A Sanctified Memory Lane

Upon the lane where memories dwell,
In sacred whispers, the stories tell.
Of prayers uttered in times of need,
Faithful hearts sowing every seed.

Each step reveals a holy trace,
A path well worn, of grace embraced.
In twilight's glow, the past returns,
With every flame, a spirit burns.

The laughter shared, the tears we shed,
In unity, our hearts are led.
For in our souls, sweet echoes play,
A symphony of yesterday.

From sorrow's depth to joy's ascent,
A testament of love well spent.
We walk this road, hand in hand,
With faith our guide, through every land.

So let us tread on holy ground,
Where sacred memories can be found.
And in reflection, let us see,
The path of love that sets us free.

Celestial Harmonies in Retrospection

In realms above, where angels play,
Celestial songs invite the day.
With every note, the heavens sway,
A harmony that lights the way.

As we reflect on life's embrace,
We find the joy in every grace.
The struggles faced, the battles won,
In this grand choir, we are one.

Through trials steep and valleys deep,
In faith we find the strength we keep.
In memories sweet, our spirits soar,
A legacy of love, forever more.

The dawn of truth through shadows cast,
In every breath, the joy amassed.
We rise with hope, our hearts aligned,
A glimpse of peace, in God we find.

So let us sing, with hearts ablaze,
A chorus loud, of endless praise.
For in reflection's gentle hold,
The greatest stories yet untold.

Faith's Cornerstones in the Distant

In distant shores, where echoes ring,
The cornerstones of faith take wing.
From ancient lands, their truths abide,
A timeless guide, our sacred guide.

With every challenge, new horizons bloom,
In every heart, dispelling gloom.
Through love and trial, our spirits rise,
In unity, we touch the skies.

In quiet moments, we seek the light,
In darkest hours, we find our sight.
Each step we take, a purpose clear,
With faith unwavering, we persevere.

A legacy woven with hopes and dreams,
Through valleys low and mountain streams.
In distant whispers, we hear the call,
To trust in love, and rise above all.

Bound by the thread of cosmic grace,
We journey forth, a holy place.
In faith's embrace, we stand as one,
A tapestry of love, never undone.